THE WORLD'S GREATEST LIES

Leigh W. Rutledge

MICHAEL O'MARA
BOOKS LIMITED

First published in Great Britain in 1999 by
Michael O'Mara Books Limited
9 Lion Yard
Tremadoc Road
London SW4 7NQ

First published in the United States under the title *Would I Lie to You?* by
Leigh W.Rutledge. Copyright © Leigh W.Rutledge, 1998. Published by
arrangement with Dutton Plume, a division of Penguin Putnam Inc.

Copyright © 1998, 1999 Leigh W.Rutledge

A CIP catalogue record for this book is available from the British Library

ISBN 1–85479–427–2

1 3 5 7 9 10 8 6 4 2

Designed and typeset by Keystroke, Wolverhampton

Printed and bound in Great Britain by Cox & Wyman, Reading, Berks

Acknowledgements

For their help and suggestions, I'd like to take
a moment to thank:

Peter Borland,
Richard Donley,
Randy Fizer,
Paul Hause,
Bill Jump,
Billy Milroy,
Kari Paschall,
Jennifer Rudolph-Walsh,
Herbie Scher,
Charlotte Simmons,
Sam Staggs,
and Roger Striffler.

Hundreds of Lies for Every Occasion

Oliver North did it in front of Congress and was proud of it. Adolf Hitler did it to a nation and left more than six million victims in his wake. Joan Crawford did it to cover up her shortcomings as a parent. The Menendez brothers did it to inherit a family fortune. Nancy Reagan, Al Capone, John James Audubon, and Henry VIII all did it. Even the apostle Peter did it – and anguished over his sin. And, according to a recent national survey, the average American does it – thirteen times a day. Generally speaking, it's only certain kinds of liars we abhor, not liars as an entire class. The man who tells his hostess that dinner was wonderful, when it wasn't, hardly arouses antipathy or scorn. The wife who tells her dying husband, 'You look better today,' seems more virtuous than corrupt. And the Gentiles who protected Anne Frank and her family from the Nazis for two years seem, rather incontrovertibly, like saints. It's those who lie to protect themselves in the face of wrongdoing, those who lie for profit or out of vanity, the politicians, policemen, celebrities, and criminals who lie to manipulate and maintain power – those are the liars we find contemptible, laughable, outrageous, dangerous. We may find it easy to forgive a movie star's foible of deducting three or four years from his or her age; but we find it understandably difficult to exonerate the senator who plays us for fools by lying about how much of our tax money went to finance his most recent golf junket to Florida.

People have always lied. The average Roman probably lied just as much about his wealth, his influence at work, or the size of his barge as the average American does today about his salary, his influence at work, and the petrol mileage of his car. It often seems as if we live in an era more awash in lies and liars than ever before. But the fact is, we probably just hear about the lies more, thanks to television, radio, the newspapers, and computers. The first book of the Old Testament, for example, is brimming with lies and liars. (Think of Cain, to name just one.) And the ancient Greeks lied when they seduced the Trojans into thinking that a huge wooden horse was a gift of peace, when in fact the 'gift' was full of warriors ready to draw their swords and make war. There may have been no stock portfolios, IQ scores, or golf handicaps to lie about in ancient China; but it's a pretty safe bet the ancient Chinese found plenty of areas in their lives ripe for trifling with the truth: sexual prowess, the price of a bronze knife, a concubine's beauty.

This book is a comic opera of the centuries – and like all comic operas, it consists of equal portions of buffoonery, tragedy, ineptitude, and horror. Its cast includes gangsters, tyrants, faded beauty queens, forgers, presidents, playwrights, serial killers, spies, athletes, first ladies, would-be Russian princesses, entire nations – as well as ordinary people caught in the act. By puffing them all together – murderous dictators next to acclaimed concert violinists, paedophiles next to movie stars – I intend no criticism, no verdict or adjudication. I leave the final judgment, as all good comic operas do, to God.

———— ◆◆◆ ————

"Whatever satisfies the soul is truth."

– Walt Whitman

'SECOND-HAND FURNITURE DEALER'

– Profession printed on Al Capone's
business cards

'The Sudetenland is the last territorial claim I have to make in Europe.'

– German Chancellor Adolf Hitler, assuring the world in 1938 that all he wanted was a little piece of Czechoslovakia; less than a year later, he invaded Poland and ignited World War II

'I have no weakness for shoes. I wear very simple shoes.'

– Former first lady of the Philippines Imelda Marcos; after the fall of her husband's dictatorship in 1986, more than 3,400 pairs of shoes – most of them far from 'simple' – were discovered in her closets at Malacanang Palace

※

Perhaps best known for her multiple marriages ('Darling, I'm a wonderful housekeeper – every time I get a divorce, I keep the house'), former Hungarian beauty queen and occasional actress Zsa Zsa Gabor went on trial in 1990 for assaulting a police officer, driving without a valid licence, and having an open container of alcohol in her vehicle. The charges stemmed from an incident in which Gabor had slapped a Beverly Hills officer after he pulled her over for having expired registration tags on her Rolls-Royce. At the trial, Gabor claimed the bourbon in her glove compartment belonged to her husband and that her registration was expired only because she had overpaid the amount, resulting in a bureaucratic snafu. As for her driver's licence – which had been visibly altered to show her year of birth as 1928 instead of 1923 (and which showed her weight as a mere 110 pounds) – Gabor insisted the licence had been stolen by illegal Mexican immigrants who inexplicably altered it to show her as younger and thinner, and then just as inexplicably returned it. After she was found guilty of the charges against her, Gabor vilified the jury. 'They were not my class of people,' she told reporters. 'There was not a producer, a press agent, a director, an actor. . . . In Nazi Hungary, they were fairer than here.'

In 1959, Liberace sued the London *Daily Mirror* and one of its journalists for libel, for implying that he was a homosexual. The *Mirror* had run a concert review in which the flamboyant pianist was referred to as 'mincing,' 'sniggering,' 'quivering,' and 'fruit-flavoured.' On the witness stand, Liberace flatly denied he was a homosexual and stated unequivocally that he had never in his life indulged in homosexual practices. The trial lasted only six days, and Liberace won the suit and a $24,000 settlement. Throughout the next thirty years, Liberace continued to deny his homosexuality publicly, even going so far as to claim he had lost his virginity to a 'hunk of woman' named Miss Bea Haven. 'In public,' said one of his former male lovers, 'he would go to any length to deny [his sexuality].' When Liberace died of AIDS in 1987, his homosexuality – an open secret in the entertainment industry – became widely known. The London *Daily Mirror* contacted the entertainer's estate and asked, unsuccessfully, for its $24,000 back.

know who broke the vase . . . It's a matter of

'No one in the White House staff, no one in this administration, presently employed, was involved in this very bizarre incident.'

– President Richard Nixon, lying to the American public at the outset of the Watergate scandal, 1972

'I was not lying. I said things that later on seemed to be untrue.'

– Former President Nixon, four years after the Watergate scandal drove him from office, 1978

were so good, I'm not even going to charge you

After Warner Brothers Studios put Humphrey Bogart under contract in the 1930s, it tried to enhance his mystique by publicly claiming he had been born on December 25, Christmas Day. In fact, the actor's birthday was January 23.

'Attention! You are in a transit camp from which you will be sent to a labour camp. In order to avoid epidemics, you must present your clothing and belongings for immediate disinfection. Gold, money, foreign currency, and jewellery should be deposited with the cashiers in return for a receipt. They will be returned to you later when you present the receipt. Bodily cleanliness requires that everyone bathe before continuing the journey.'

weeks . . . But I just filled the petrol tank . . .

– Sign posted at the train depot in the concentration camp Treblinka, to alleviate the fears of arriving Jews and expedite their movement into the gas chambers

🜔

'ARBEIT MACHT FREI'

– Sign posted above the entrance to every
Nazi concentration camp; it means
'Work Shall Make You Free'

---

by a little old lady who only drove it once a

'The [Cuban] movement is not a Communist movement. . . . We have no intention of expropriating U.S. property, and any property we take we'll pay for.'

– Communist revolutionary Fidel Castro, lying to U.S. diplomats about his intentions after seizing control of Cuba in 1959

In 1971, New York publisher McGraw-Hill announced the acquisition of the decade: the intimate memoirs of reclusive billionaire Howard Hughes, as told to a then little-known writer, Clifford Irving. Irving claimed to have recorded more than a hundred hours of Hughes's reminiscences, and backed up his claim with convincing letters and legal documents, all apparently in Hughes's handwriting. McGraw-Hill proudly asserted, 'We have a completely convincing manuscript; no one who has read it can doubt its integrity, or, upon reading it, the integrity of Clifford Irving.' Their confidence was misplaced. Just a month after the initial announcement, Hughes himself broke his legendary seclusion and held a press conference, via telephone, from his penthouse in Las Vegas. He denounced the entire project as a fraud. Subsequent investigation proved that Irving had forged all of the correspondence with Hughes and that he and a friend – children's author Richard Suskind – had fabricated the entire 1,200-page Hughes autobiography (for which they received a $765,000 advance). Irving subsequently spent seventeen months in prison as a result of the hoax.

town . . . Aw, hell, I coulda knocked him cold

During the 1950s, the U.S. government and the Atomic Energy Commission repeatedly lied to civilians about the dangers of above-ground nuclear testing in the Nevada desert. After a radioactive cloud passed directly over the city of Las Vegas in 1951, one government official tried to quell near-panic among local residents by claiming that the cloud was nothing more than an everyday weather phenomenon, the result of 'smoke accumulated by inversion.' Five years later, the Atomic Energy Commission asserted that beef cattle raised in the areas of heaviest fallout were 'quite safe for food' and that above-ground tests could be conducted every week 'for an indefinite period' without endangering the local population; the commission claimed that radiation from the nuclear blasts was no more hazardous than 'wearing a luminous-dial wristwatch.' One Atomic Energy Commission report even tried to persuade southern Nevada residents how lucky they were; in a study of the effects of intense radiation on insects, the AEC asserted, 'Fruit flies raised for 128 generations in highly radioactive surroundings did not degenerate as expected. Instead, they ended up a better race of fruit flies – hardier, more vigorous, more reproductive, with better resistance to disease.'

॥

During the 1995 criminal trial of O.J. Simpson on charges of murdering his ex-wife, Nicole, and her friend Ronald Goldman, L.A. detective Mark Fuhrman – who had gathered much of the crime scene evidence against Simpson – was questioned carefully about his attitudes toward African-Americans and whether he was, as some people alleged, a racist.

'Do you use the word 'nigger' in describing people?' asked defence lawyer F. Lee Bailey.

'No, sir.' said Fuhrman.

'Have you used that word in the past ten years?'

'Not that I recall, no.'

'Is it possible that you have forgotten that act on your part?'

No, it is not possible.'

'And you say under oath that you have not addressed any black person as a 'nigger' or spoken about black people as 'niggers' in the past ten years?'

'That's what I'm saying, sir.

Six months later, Fuhrman was forced to return to the stand, to answer questions about tapes showing he had indeed used the word, no less than 41 times, in interviews from 1985 to 1994 with would-be screenwriter Laura Hart McKinney, who was writing a script about women police officers. This time, when questioned under oath, a haggard and defensive-looking Fuhrman pleaded the Fifth. He was later charged with perjury and sentenced to three years probation.

'Not a cough in a carload.'

– Advertising tag line used in the 1950s
by Old Gold cigarettes

Lightning never strikes twice in the same place

Contrary to popular belief, lightning does
sometimes strike the same object twice.
Although a comparatively rare phenomenon,
it most frequently occurs when the second
bolt follows the first within seconds.

The Vatican has the largest collection of pornography in the world

The world's largest collection of pornography actually resides at the Kinsey Institute in Bloomington, Indiana U.S.A. The institute – which is devoted to sex research and education – owns more than 100,000 pieces of erotica, including books, photographs, films, sculptures, and explicitly erotic works by numerous famous artists. By comparison, the Vatican probably does not even have a substantive collection of pornography. Although a definitive inventory of its holdings is unknown, the Church holds an exhaustive collection of art by Michelangelo, Raphael, and others (some of which, depending on the definition, might be considered erotic), file copies of all the books on the Vatican's Index of Forbidden Books (most of which were forbidden because of blasphemy and heresy, not obscenity), and many rare and priceless books (some of which may be incidentally pornographic in nature).

Lana Turner was discovered by a film producer at Schwab's Drugstore in Hollywood

Actually, Turner was first noticed by a journalist for the Hollywood Reporter (who suggested she go to one of the studios for a screen test) at Currie's Ice Cream Parlour, across the street from Hollywood High School.

———◆◆◆———

Dresden china comes from Dresden, Germany

In fact, Dresden china has not been manufactured in Dresden since 1710. For the last 290 years, it's been made in Meissen, a town several miles to the northwest.

It's dangerous to swim less than an hour after eating

According to the Red Cross, it may be *uncomfortable* to swim within an hour after eating, but the old folklore that it leads to stomach cramps and thus drowning is untrue.

Coffee stunts your growth

There is no indication that coffee consumption at any age affects one's growth one way or the other.

Mussolini made the trains run on time

According to many of those who lived in Italy during the entire twenty-three-year dictatorship of Benito Mussolini, from 1922 to 1945, Italian trains were rarely on schedule.

———◆◆———

Mama Cass choked to death on a ham sandwich

The hefty singer – of the popular 1960s group the Mamas and the Papas – actually died of a massive heart attack. Although her obesity was a major contributing factor to her death, she was not eating at the time of the attack.

In the fall of 1990, students and faculty at Coronado High School in Colorado Springs welcomed a pretty new female transfer student, Cheyen Weatherly, to their campus. Cheyen – a bright-eyed and gregarious young woman – had recently moved to the area with her family from Greece. She soon distinguished herself as a very popular girl; she even made the all-girl cheerleading squad. The only problem was, Cheyen Weatherly was a twenty-six-year-old man named Charles Dougherty. Dougherty's impersonation escaped detection until school officials suddenly discovered that all of Cheyen Weatherly's

put on a few pounds . . . I didn't mean to . . .

background records were fictitious. (One six-teen-year-old classmate claimed to have been suspicious all along. 'He had a lot of makeup on' she said. 'It looked like it was plastered.') After being arrested on charges of criminal impersonation, Dougherty was diagnosed as having a multiple personality disorder. His case created an uproar of indignation in the largely conservative community, but – despite the demands of outraged parents, some of whom even suggested he receive the death penalty – he was sentenced to two years' probation, with the qualification he undergo psychiatric counselling.

———◆◆◆———

'I have here in my hand a list of 205, a list of names that were known to the Secretary of State as being members of the Communist Party and who nevertheless are still working and shaping the policy of the State Department.'

– Wisconsin Republican Senator Joseph McCarthy, waving what may have actually been a shopping list, in front of a Republican women's club meeting in 1950; McCarthy's announcement, meant to stir up interest in his sagging political career, led to unprecedented government witch hunts for Communists during the next four years, resulting in the ruined careers and lives of hundreds of innocent people

to walk . . . I dropped out of school because it

'Perhaps it could have come from . . . using coal, the kind for heating material, during winter.'

– A Soviet official in 1986, lying to the world about why there were suddenly very high levels of radioactivity all over Europe; unbeknownst to the outside world, the Soviet nuclear power plant at Chernobyl was in the process of melting down

——◆◆◆——

Silent screen star Theda Bara –
known as the Vamp, for her exotic
portrayals of heartless femme
fatales – regularly claimed to have
been the illegitimate offspring of
a French painter and his beautiful
Egyptian concubine; she said she
had been born in the middle
of the Sahara Desert. In fact,
Miss Bara was born in Cincinnati,
Ohio, the daughter of a tailor
and his wife. Her real last
name was Goodman.

. . . If you'll just do this one thing for me,

1. Sacheen Littlefeather

'Hello. My name is Sacheen Littlefeather.
I'm Apache, and I am president of the National
Native American Affirmative Image
Committee.' With those introductory words,
a slender and pretty young woman, dressed in
white buckskin and an exotic leather headdress,
stunned the 1972 Academy Awards ceremony.
Littlefeather had been sent by Marlon Brando
to refuse his Best Actor Oscar for his widely
acclaimed performance as Don Corleone in
The Godfather. Brando, she explained, 'very
regretfully cannot accept this very generous
award. And the reason for this is the treatment
of American Indians today by the film industry
and on television.' Littlefeather's speech – one of
the first instances of using the Oscars ceremony
as a political podium – was greeted with catcalls
and unhappy murmurs from the star-studded

audience. 'I beg,' she said in conclusion, sounding suspiciously like an actress portraying an Indian maiden in an old western, 'that I have not intruded upon this evening and that we will, in the future, in our hearts and our understanding, meet with love and generosity.' Brando's refusal of the Academy Award made international headlines the next morning. The headlines turned slightly amused several days later when gossip columnist Liz Smith revealed that 'Sacheen Littlefeather' – despite her memorable costume and slightly halting speech – was really a struggling Hollywood starlet named Maria Cruz, who had been crowned Miss American Vampire of 1970 two years earlier. Whether or not Cruz had any Apache blood in her was never precisely ascertained by the media. She went on to achieve even more notoriety six months after the Academy Awards ceremony when she posed nude for *Playboy* magazine.

2. Sebastian Melmouth

In 1897, after his release from prison – where he had served a gruelling two years of hard labour for having commited homosexual acts – the once-celebrated playwright Oscar Wilde fled England and settled in Paris, where he remained in exile until his death three years later. In order to avoid further scandal or unpleasantness, he adopted the fictitious name 'Sebastian Melmouth.' Even his luggage was mono-grammed 'S.M.' The incognito proved absurd, however: Everyone knew who he was. The tall, physically imposing playwright, with long brown locks and a flamboyant manner, cut a readily identifiable figure on any street. (Immediately after his release from prison, he stood in a train station admiring flowers and exclaimed, 'Oh, beautiful world! Oh, beautiful world!' One of his travelling companions admonished him, 'Now, Mr. Wilde, you mustn't give yourself away like that. You're the only man in England who would talk like that in a railway station.') Exiled in Paris, Wilde often complained to friends that, as the central figure in one of the nineteenth-century's most notorious scandals, he was as recognizable as the Eiffel Tower.

3. Anne Rice

The bestselling author was actually born Howard Allen O'Brien. In regard to her unusual first name, Rice has explained that her parents wanted a son.

☿

4. Mata Hari

The legendary dancer and courtesan – later accused of being a German spy during World War I – actually started life as a Dutch house-wife, with the name Margaretha Zelle. She took the stage name Mata Hari when she decided to pursue a dancing career in Paris. It's generally thought that the sudden death of her only son, plus years of physical and emotional abuse at the hands of her husband, were the catalysts for her determined self-transformation into one of the most exotic figures in early twentieth-century Europe.

5. Honoré de Balzac

The great French novelist (1799–1850) added 'de' to his name as an affectation and tried to pass himself off as a member of the French aristocracy. In fact, he was the son of a minor civil servant who had come from peasant stock in southern France.

6. Daniel Defoe

The renowned English novelist – best known as the author of *Robinson Crusoe* – also added 'de' to his name in order to make it sound more impressive. He had been born, simply, Daniel Foe.

7. Mrs. Theresa Neele

In December 1926, a slightly overweight and vaguely tired-looking woman in her late thirties registered at a fashionable English health spa, The Hydro. She signed herself as 'Mrs. Theresa Neele.' According to other guests at the hotel, she seemed 'normal and happy.' She socialized freely, played billiards, went dancing in the evenings, sometimes took long walks, and could often be seen in the parlour reading newspapers. She was, from all accounts, a perfectly typical hotel visitor. On the tenth day of her stay, a handsome man, also in his thirties, approached her for conversation as she sat perusing the evening papers. She looked up at him as if she knew him, but, according to a witness, 'She only seemed to regard him as an acquaintance whose identity she could not quite fix.' He led her into the dining room for further conversation. A short time later, he released a long-awaited statement to the press: 'There is no question about the identity. It is my wife. She has suffered from the most complete loss of memory and I do not think she knows who she is.' The woman in question was the immensely popular mystery writer Agatha Christie, who had disappeared from her home without a trace a week and a half earlier. Her sudden disappearance set off a nationwide manhunt: Newspapers offered huge rewards for clues to her whereabouts, civilians combed the countryside in search of her, lakes and ponds were dragged for her corpse. The actual circumstances of Christie's disappearance remain a mystery to this day. Although she later claimed to have been stricken with total amnesia as a result of paralyzing grief over her mother's death, in reality her husband, Archibald, had recently told her he was in love with another woman and wanted a divorce. Some observers have speculated that Christie, in an emotional daze, vanished in order to spite him. Perhaps tellingly, the name of the other woman (who would, in fact, eventually become Archibald's second wife) was Miss Nancy Neele.

8. Forrest Carter

To tens of thousands of eager readers in the 1970s and 1980s, the books of Forrest Carter were exciting, even inspirational. His first successful novel, *The Rebel Outlaw: Josey Wales*, was made into a popular movie starring Clint Eastwood in 1976. That same year, Carter brought out a charming and poignant memoir of his early life growing up as a Native American, *The Education of Little Tree*, which eventually rose to No.1 on the *New York Times* paperback nonfiction bestseller list. In publicity interviews, Carter portrayed himself as a Cherokee cowboy, a self-taught writer. It wasn't until the late 1980s that the truth about Carter and his life came out: He was neither Cherokee nor a cowboy. He was actually Asa Earl Carter, one of the most feared white supremacists in the state of Alabama, a racial zealot who had, for thirty years, been a self-styled guerrilla for the Ku Klux Klan. Among his numerous racist activities, Carter had written anti-segregation speeches (including the infamous 'Segregation now, segregation tomorrow, segregation forever' speech) for George Wallace, and in the 1950s he was indicted for assault with intent to murder after a violent argument over money with two fellow Klansmen. In stark contrast to the inspiring, deeply spiritual life of the entirely fictitious Forrest Carter, Asa was closely associated with a notorious Birmingham-based organization that had been responsible for the castration of a young African-American and the violent disruption of Nat King Cole concerts in the 1950s. Said a researcher from Emory University, 'The carefully constructed mask of Forrest Carter – Cherokee cowboy, self-taught writer, and spokesman for the American Indian – was simply the last fantasy of a man who reinvented himself again and again. . . . This guru of new-age environmentalists was actually a gun-toting racist.' Despite the revelations, *The Education of Little Tree* was made into a critically acclaimed film in 1997.

Real name

Julie Andrews	*Julia Elizabeth Wells*
Andy Warhol	*Andrew Warhola*
Whoopi Goldberg	*Caryn Johnson*
Rodney Dangerfield	*Jacob Cohen*
Stevie Wonder	*Steveland Morris* Hardaway
Bo Derek	*Mary Cathleen Collins*
Charlton Heston	*Charles Carter*
Audrey Hepburn	*Edna Ruston*
John le Carré	*David John Cornwell*
Roy Rogers	*Leonard Slye*
Ben Kingsley	*Krishna Bhanji*
Axl Rose	*William Bailey*
Sting	*Gordon Sumner*
Abigail Van Buren	*Pauline Friedman*
Jane Seymour	*Joyce Penelope Frankenberg*
'Legs' Diamond	*John T. Nolan*
Harry Houdini	*Ehrich Weiss*
Sugar Ray Robinson	*Walker Smith*

After Saddam Hussein invaded Kuwait in 1990, the U.S. Congress held public hearings to determine what, if anything, the U.S. response should be. Among those who testified at the hearings was a tearful Kuwaiti girl – known only as 'Nayirah' – who devastated spectators with her eyewitness accounts of Iraqi soldiers storming through hospitals, yanking Kuwaiti babies from their incubators, and then dumping the infants in dustbins. The story inflamed the American public, including President Bush, who often cited it when justifying his decision to 'liberate' Kuwait and enter the Gulf War. Shortly after the war ended, however, it was revealed that 'Nayirah' – far from being an objective eye-witness of war atrocities – was none other than the daughter of Kuwait's ambassador to the United States. Not only had she never personally witnessed any atrocities by Iraqi soldiers, but she hadn't even been in her country at any time in the recent past. It further came out that while numerous infants did indeed die in hospitals during the first days of the Iraqi occupation, the reason was that an estimated 90 percent of Kuwaiti doctors fled their posts in order to sit out the war in neighbouring, friendly countries.

film and we expect to hear from Fox and

'I'm a very nonviolent person.'

– Serial killer Ted Bundy, after his arrest in
Florida in 1979; Bundy – who was responsible
for the grisly murders of as many as three dozen
girls and young women in four different states
– was executed in the Florida electric chair
in 1989

American writer Horatio Alger (1834–1899) was best known for his 'rags to riches' boys' novels, in which earnest, hardworking orphans became admirable, wealthy gentlemen through honesty and perseverance. His books were among the top-selling novels of the late nineteenth-century. Alger himself was a tireless philanthropist working to improve conditions for homeless youths, orphans, and runaways. He was also homosexual, with a penchant for teenage boys; in fact, he was once run out of Brewster, Massachusetts – where he was pastor of the local Unitarian church – for his sexual involvement with some of the village youths. Herbert Mayes's 'definitive' biography of Alger, published in 1928, made no mention of Alger's homosexuality, but instead portrayed him as a fun-loving heterosexual with a taste for fast women. Maye's biography was the standard reference on Alger's life for over sixty years. However, in the early 1970's, Mayes confessed that the entire biography had been a fabrication, that he had completely censored the true facts of Alger's life and had invented the existence of a Horatio Alger diary that the biography was supposedly based on. So widely accepted were Mayes' lies about Alger that, as late as 1974, the *Encyclopaedia Britannica* was still reiterating them in its entry on Alger.

———◆—◆———

'"George," said his father, "do you know who killed this beautiful little cherry tree yonder in the garden?" . . . "I can't tell a lie, Pa; you know I can't tell a lie. I did cut it with my hatchet."'

– From an 1806 biography of George Washington; the story of George and the cherry tree, taught as fact to generations of schoolchildren, was a complete fabrication, the invention of early Washington biographer Mason Weems, who contrived endless anecdotes about Washington to fill in what he was too lazy to research

before in my life . . . I've told you everything I

'Maybe the food didn't agree with them.'

– Boardinghouse keeper Delfina Gonzalez, lying to Mexico City police about the more than fifty bodies discovered buried in her yard; it turned out Delfina and her sister had been running an illegal brothel for years and routinely murdered the prostitutes to avoid detection; the two were arrested in 1964

know . . . You haven't changed one bit . . . This

Exhausted by ten years of unsuccessfully laying siege to the city of Troy, the ancient Greeks conceived the subterfuge of building a large hollow wooden horse, hiding their best soldiers within it, and then offering the horse as a token of peace to the Trojans. Despite some initial wariness ('Do you think they have gone?' cried one suspicious citizen. 'Do you think that any gifts of the Greeks lack treachery?'), the Trojans eventually allowed the horse inside their city walls. The concealed Greek warriors then poured out and led a vicious assault on the city, leaving most of the Trojan men dead and the women enslaved.

An Olympic gold medalist in track and field during the 1930s, Stella Walsh was considered one of the most formidable woman runners in the world. She won a total of nine Olympic medals, five of them gold. Later, she married and retired to a suburb of Cleveland, where she devoted herself to working with children in athletics. To the people who knew her, it came as a terrible shock when, in 1981, she was mugged and shot to death in a department store parking lot. It came as an even bigger shock when, during preparations for the funeral, it was discovered that Stella Walsh had all along been a man. Born Stanislawa Walaslewicz in Poland in 1911, Walsh had often aroused comment during competition in the 1930s with her extraordinary musculature and excessive body hair; it was often remarked that she ran like a man. In 1956, after retiring from competition, Walsh married car salesman Harry Olson in Las Vegas; they separated after eight weeks but never divorced. After Walsh's death, Olson said he was surprised by the revelation of his wife's true sex. He told the press that he and Walsh had had sex only 'a couple of times. . . . And she wouldn't let me have the lights on.' Despite the revelation that Walsh was a man, the U.S. Olympic Committee announced there would be no attempt to post-humously rescind her Olympic medals.

'I didn't inhale it.'

– Presidential candidate Bill Clinton, trying
to exercise damage control after a previous
acknowledgement that he had 'experimented
once or twice' with marijuana in college, 1992

Former First Lady Nancy Reagan has routinely lied about her age in public, traditionally deducting two years from the truth. College and high school records list the year of her birth as 1921; her staff, however, has been instructed to tell the media that she was born in 1923. In 1988, the White House held a much-publicized party to celebrate Mrs. Reagan's sixty-fifth birthday. She was, in fact, sixty-seven.

'Come see for yourself!' proclaimed the full-page ad in the April 10, 1985, *New York Times*. 'The living unicorn! Only at Ringling Bros. and Barnum & Bailey Circus!' In fact, there were four 'unicorns' performing at the circus: white, gentle-looking creatures the size of ponies, with a single large horn growing out of the centre of their heads. The hype surrounding these previously in-mythology-only animals soon aroused the suspicion of the A.S.P.C.A. and the New York State Department of Agriculture. A state veterinarian was sent out to investigate, and ascertained that the endearing creatures under the Big Top were not unicorns at all, but goats, surgically altered to produce a single horn from the middle of their foreheads. Although no charges were filed against the circus – in fact, the animals were found to be very well taken care of – a doctor from the A.S.P.C.A. raised larger questions of medical ethics: 'You can say it's fun and let's keep the fantasy going, but think of the implications. This year it's a unicorn. Next year, someone may decide to play around with eye sockets and make a Cyclops. Where do we stop?'

Moviegoers in 1956 were thrilled and astonished by the previously unsuspected purity and beauty of Deborah Kerr's singing voice in the film version of Rodgers and Hammerstein's *The King and I*. Who knew that the charming Miss Kerr could sing as well as act? Likewise, five years later, it came as a surprise to many when Natalie Wood acquitted herself as well as she did in the demanding musical role of Maria in the film *West Side Story*. What audiences didn't know or even suspect at the time was that they weren't hearing Deborah Kerr or Natalie Wood sing at all – they were hearing the voice of Marni Nixon, the most famous 'ghost' singer in

can get you diamonds at below wholesale . . .

Hollywood history. Born Marni McEathron in 1929, Nixon made a career of dubbing Hollywood musicals when the stars themselves weren't up to the challenge. In 1964, she dubbed the singing voice of Audrey Hepburn in the popular film *My Fair Lady*. (Hepburn initially underwent several months of voice training for the role; but at the last minute producers decided to have her singing dubbed by Nixon, a decision that infuriated Hepburn.) Nixon herself appeared on-screen only once in her movie career: as a nun in the film *The Sound of Music* in 1965.

'They were inventions, nothing was true. . . . There is nothing true about those allegations. They are as untrue as everything else that these people have been telling in the past.'

– Former UN Secretary General Kurt Waldheim, lying about his Nazi past during his campaign to become president of Austria in 1986; Waldheim's official biography stated he was wounded in World War II in 1941 and then resumed law studies in Vienna; the World Jewish Congress found documents showing that Waldheim was in fact part of a Nazi unit involved in war atrocities during the years when he was supposedly studying

offer . . . I've got a headache tonight . . . I was

14 MEMORABLE QUOTES ABOUT LYING

'That's not a lie, it's a terminological inexactitude.'

– Former U.S. Secretary of State Alexander Haig, defending himself against accusations of lying, 1983

'The whole question of lying to Congress – you could call it a lie, but for us, that's keeping cover.'

– Former CIA Agent David Whipple

———◆◆◆———

'People tell about two lies a day, or at least that is how many they will admit to.'

– Psychologist Bella DePaulo

'Lying increases the creative faculties, expands the ego, lessens the friction of social contacts. . . . It is only in lies, wholeheartedly and bravely told, that human nature attains through words and speech the forebearance, the nobility, the romance, the idealism that . . . it falls so short of in fact and deed.'

– Clare Boothe Luce

'I think I lie pretty effectively.'

– O.J. Simpson, 1969

'Since when is a commercial supposed to be accurate?'

– An official of the Republican National Committee, indignantly responding to charges that a 1984 reelection ad for Ronald Reagan wasn't just hedging the truth but lying outright

been able to wear a size 10 before . . .

'Since politicians don't believe what they say, they are surprised when the people believe what they say.'

– Charles de Gaulle

———◆◆◆———

'He who speaks the truth must have one foot in the stirrup.'

– Armenian proverb

'You made your bed, now lie about it.'

– Attributed to Mrs. Loring, mother of renowned New York City art connoisseur Jack Loring

———◆◆◆———

'I wasn't lying, Senator. I was presenting a different version from the facts.'

– Oliver North, at the Iran-Contra hearings in 1987

'If I blunder; everyone can notice it; not so, if I lie.'

– Goethe

'There is nothing so pathetic as a forgetful liar.'

– F.M. Knowles

'If you think fishermen are the biggest liars in the world, ask a jogger how far he runs in the morning.'

– Larry Johnson

———◆◆◆———

'The most convincing way to tell a lie is to tell the truth and make it sound like a lie.'

– Mark Twain

**'I ran the race. I really did.
I feel like I went more
than twenty-six miles.'**

– Rosie Ruiz, winner of the women's division
of the 1980 Boston Marathon; shortly after
winning, Ruiz was stripped of her title when it
was discovered she hadn't run the entire course
at all but had jumped into the race a half-mile
before the finish line. 'I saw a woman stumble
out of the crowd,' said one eyewitness. 'She
looked like she wasn't a runner. Her arms
were flying around. . . . I didn't take her very
seriously.'

'ELVIS SEEN IN MIAMI SUPERMARKET!'

– Headline in supermarket tabloid, the *Weekly World News*, April 28, 1981, four years after Presley's death

Perhaps the greatest art forger of the twentieth century, Elmyr de Hory painted dozens of fake Picassos, Matisses, and Modiglianis, which for years deceived many of the best art dealers and museums in the world. The total market value of his counterfeit output was once estimated at over $60 million, and some of his forgeries are believed to still be hanging in reputable galleries and prestigious collections. Since his death, he has been acknowledged by art historians as 'a genius of sorts.' Born in Budapest in 1906, de Hory began to show some artistic talent in his mid-teens and was sent to study at the prestigious Akademie Heimann in Munich, where he received rigorous training in drawing. From there he went to Paris, where he studied with the famous French painter Fernand Léger. De Hory had ambitions to become a renowned painter himself, but despite an occasional exhibition, his work was generally greeted with indifference, and he relied on a steady stream of money from his wealthy parents to make ends meet. When the Nazis occupied Hungary, the de Hory family fortune was confiscated, and Elmyr suddenly found himself broke and struggling in Paris. Then one afternoon, a wealthy friend and art collector, Lady Malcolm Campbell, visited his studio and noticed what she thought was an unsigned Picasso hanging on the wall. It was actually a drawing that de Hory himself had dashed off in ten minutes one rainy afternoon when he was bored. De Hory did nothing to disabuse Lady Campbell of the work's authenticity, and when she offered him a large sum of money to buy it, he sold it to her. Later, after he learned she'd resold the work to a reputable London art dealer for a sizable profit, he immediately went to work and produced several more 'Picassos,' which he then sold to a dealer in Paris for $400. For the next two decades, de Hory produced paintings, drawings, and gouaches 'by' Matisse, Renoir, Picasso, Modigliani, Dufy, and Braque. To sell his forgeries, he employed a variety of disguises and false identities. When word got around to 'watch out for a suave fifty-year-old Hungarian with a monocle in his eye and a Matisse under his arm,' de Hory simply changed his name and his appearance, and began marketing his wares in a new location. He was once literally chased out of a gallery in Beverly Hills by a dealer who spotted his works as forgeries, but generally he managed to deceive experts around the world. He sold a forged Matisse to the Fogg Art Museum at Harvard University (only after years of painstaking investigation did they finally conclude it was a fake); another 'Matisse' was praised internationally as a masterpiece and sold for more than $60,000. De Hory was amazed when he would pick up an art book and discover one of his forgeries reproduced as an 'exceptional' Picasso or Modigliani. Eventually, de Hory linked up with two other men, Fernand Legros and Real Lessard, who were unscrupulous Paris art dealers. They persuaded de Hory to mass-produce dozens of forgeries, which they could then peddle around the world for tens of thousands of dollars. Because the works often needed letters of authenticity before museums would buy them, they once sent one of de Hory's best Picassos to Picasso himself. Picasso, of course, didn't remember having painted it; but then again, he didn't remember not painting it, either. Finally, when he was told it had been valued at $100,000, the great artist remarked, 'Well then, it must be real,' and he authenticated the work. The successful forgery ring was finally exposed in 1967 when a Texas millionaire, who had bought forty-four of the fakes, realized he was being defrauded and went to the police. (One journalist later dubbed him 'the man who owns what may be the largest private collection of fake paintings in the world.') For nine years after that, de Hory managed to elude authorities and stay out of prison. Finally, in 1976, his arrest seemed imminent. Rather than face imprisonment at the age of seventy, the master of forgery committed suicide with a lethal overdose of barbiturates.

〽

'I'm behind him 1,000 percent.'

– 1972 Democratic presidential candidate
George McGovern, expressing support for his
running mate, Thomas Eagleton, after the press
revealed that Eagleton had once undergone
electroshock treatments for depression; a
few days later, McGovern dumped him

〽

'I have called this press conference to label as false and scurrilous and malicious these rumours, these assertions and accusations. I'm labelling them as damned lies.'

– Vice-President of the United States Spiro Agnew, denying that he ever received kickbacks and bribes from building contractors when he had been governor of Maryland; two months after his heated public denials, in the face of overwhelming evidence of his guilt, Agnew pleaded 'no contest' to related charges; he resigned the vice presidency in disgrace on October 10, 1973

'The only thing I have done is carry a pistol into a movie. . . . I haven't done anything to be ashamed of. . . . I didn't kill anybody . . . I haven't shot anybody. . . . '

– Lee Harvey Oswald, to Dallas police, during his arrest in a Dallas movie theatre, November 22, 1963 the day JFK was shot

In the late spring of 1926, the sudden, mysterious disappearance of popular evangelist and faith healer Aimee Semple McPherson stunned the nation. She had last been seen by her secretary sitting by the southern California ocean working on a new sermon. There were few leads and few clues. When news of the disappearance was made public, her legions of followers were beside themselves. One committed suicide. Two of them drowned while frantically searching the Pacific Ocean for her body. The others, numbering in the thousands, camped along the shoreline waiting for word of her fate. McPherson – founder of the Foursquare Church and known for her theatrical style of preaching (she once rode a police motorcycle down the aisle of her church to deliver a sermon on law and order) – was finally presumed dead from drowning. A memorial service – sans the deceased – was held on June 20; but then, just a few days later, Sister Aimee reappeared as

times . . . It's not your body I'm attracted to, it's

mysteriously and abruptly as she had vanished. She was discovered in a Mexican border town, Aqua Prieta, and claimed to have been kidnapped, tortured, and held captive by bandits for a month in the hostile Sonora Desert of Mexico. The fact that her clothes were in pristine condition – and she looked as radiant and healthy as ever – aroused suspicion in some quarters. 'My story is true!' she retorted defensively. 'Why should I lie? What motive would I have? What would I have to gain?' She even posed for a series of photographs reenacting her terrifying ordeal, including one that showed exactly how she had cut through ropes around her wrists using the jagged edge of a metal can. The Los Angeles district attorney's office, however, didn't believe a word of it, and by the time their investigation was complete they discovered that Aimee had spent the missing month not as the hostage of unknown, ruthless kidnappers, but rather in a secret romantic interlude with a married radio engineer, Kenneth Ormiston, in an idyllic seaside cottage near

Carmel, California. Although many of her followers remained loyal to her, Aimee's reputation and evangelical work suffered for the sex scandal. Her revivalist activities continued, however, for almost another twenty years, before she died, at the age of fifty-four, from an accidental overdose of sleeping pills.

———◆◆◆———

'We do not have censorship. What we have is a limitation of what newspapers can report.'

– The South African Deputy Minister for Information, 1987

Of the various actors – including Peter Ustinov, Sidney Toler, and Peter Sellers – who have portrayed detective Charlie Chan in the movies and on television, not a single one has been of Chinese descent.

'I'd never withhold love from my children. That's why I wanted them, to give them love. . . . There are plenty of people who have thought me too loving.'

– Joan Crawford

'Of all the treasures a State can possess, the human lives of its citizens are for us the most precious.'

– Soviet dictator Joseph Stalin; between 1930 and 1938, Stalin slaughtered an estimated 20 million to 40 million Soviet citizens through a reign of terror that included mass executions and purposely induced famines (to punish uncooperative regions of the country)

'The culture of Democratic Kampuchea is of a national, popular, forward-looking, and healthful character.'

– From the constitution of Cambodia, rewritten in 1975 by Communist dictator Pol Pot; almost immediately after Pol Pot and his army, the Khmer Rouge, took over the country they began slaughtering the Cambodian people, until, four years later roughly two million were dead; as an example of the regime's genocidal madness, all individuals who wore eyeglasses were executed, for fear that as 'intellectuals' they might criticize the country's new leadership

'Because of unrest in the town, it has become necessary to move the family downstairs. It would be dangerous to be in the upper rooms if there was shooting in the streets.'

– Bolshevik commander Yakov Yurovsky, lying to Czar Nicholas II and his family about why, in the middle of the night, they must all go down to the basement; moments later, their official death sentence was read aloud, and the royal family was shot, stabbed, and beaten to death

'I am the daughter of the Czar of Russia.'

– Mystery woman Anna Anderson, reiterating on U.S. television in 1976 her decades-long insistence that she was Anastasia, the daughter of Czar Nicholas II; Anderson claimed to have miraculously survived the Bolshevik massacre of Nicholas and his family; despite much compelling evidence in her favour through the years, posthumous DNA tests on her tissue samples conclusively proved she was not a member of the Russian royal family

'Single gentleman, aged 45, with income of 400 per year, desires to marry homely lady of similar age and income.'

– Personals ad repeatedly placed in Paris news-papers between 1914 and 1919 by Henri Landru (otherwise known as 'Bluebeard'), who lured unsuspecting women into romantic liasons with him and then swindled them out of their money and murdered them; he was eventually caught and, after being convicted of nine of the mur-ders, was guillotined in 1922

Sir Roger Tichborne was a typical young English gentleman of the mid-nineteenth century. Slender, dark, and vaguely foppish, he was extremely well-educated, and he spoke French fluently. Perhaps the only atypical thing about him was the tattoo he sported on his left arm. In April 1854, at the age of twenty-four, he booked passage on a ship, the *Bella*, bound for Jamaica. The *Bella* never made it to her destination. The ship foundered, and all that was ever found of her was an empty lifeboat and a few pieces of wreckage floating off the coast of Brazil. Roger's mother, Lady Tichborne, refused to believe that her son had perished at sea. For more than a decade afterward she advertised in newspapers around the world hoping to receive some word of him. In 1865, she got the word: An illiterate note penned by a down-and-out Australian horse thief, Arthur Orton, who claimed to be her son. Unlike the actual Roger Tichborne, Orton was blond, obese, and spoke barely intelligible English, let alone French. He also had no tattoo on his left arm. (He claimed it must have faded.) Still, Lady Tichborne sent him money to come to Europe and, despite the glaring inconsistencies (he couldn't even tell her what her maiden name was), she eventually proclaimed him to be her long-lost son. For nearly five years after that, Orton got away with his outrageous lie and fed off the elderly woman's substantial estate. Then, in 1871, Lady Tichborne died. The rest of the family, always hostile to Orton's claims, challenged his right to any portion of the family inheritance. After a protracted and highly publicized trial, the courts concluded that Orton was not Sir Roger, and soon afterward the Australian was arrested for perjury and was tried, convicted, and sentenced to fourteen years in prison. When he died, virtually penniless, in 1898, he asked that the name 'Sir Roger Tichborne' be inscribed on his coffin.

'They shot and killed my parents! . . . My mom and dad. My mom and dad!'

– A sobbing Lyle Menendez, reporting to Beverly Hills 911, on August 20, 1989, that intruders had just murdered his wealthy parents; seven months later, Lyle and his brother, Erik, were charged with the killings, after embarking on a spending spree that all but depleted their father's $15 million estate; they were convicted in 1996

the bell . . . I was just following orders . . . I only

LIES?

**'I had no prior knowledge of
the planned assault on
Nancy Kerrigan.'**

– Olympic figure skater Tonya Harding,
suspected but never officially indicted in a
club-wielding attack on skating rival Nancy
Kerrigan, 1994

'I didn't solicit anybody.'

– Eddie Murphy, asserting that when police caught him picking up a twenty-year-old transvestite prostitute on Santa Monica Boulevard in Los Angeles at four a.m. in May 1997, he wasn't looking for sex; Murphy claimed he'd gone out to buy a newspaper and, acting as a Good Samaritan, he simply offered the prostitute a lift; the prostitute was arrested, Murphy was not

———◆◆———

'There have been many disgusting statements made recently concerning allegations of improper conduct on my part. These statements about me are totally false.'

– Michael Jackson, denying allegations that he sexually molested a twelve-year-old boy; Jackson eventually settled a lawsuit, brought by the boy's family, out of court in 1994

'The allegations in today's *Star* are not true. I have nothing to add to what I've said in the past.'

– Bill Clinton, denying published reports that, while governor of Arkansas, he had a longtime extramarital affair with state employee Gennifer Flowers, 1992

'I have more music from Chopin than from any of the others. Of course, as his music is mainly for the piano, it does make it easier to dictate his pieces to me than it is for the other composers like Beethoven.'

– British psychic Rosemary Brown, who claimed, in the 1970s, that the spirits of famous composers were dictating new compositions to her; Brown – who had had virtually no musical training-produced dozens of beautiful musical compositions which baffled a wide array of investigative musicologists

'Bearing malice in her heart against the King and following her frail and carnal lust, she did falsely and traitorously procure by means of indecent language, gifts and other arts . . . diverse of the King's daily and familiar servants to be her adulterers and concubines.'

– Indictment against Anne Boleyn, second wife of Henry VIII; Anne was falsely accused by Henry of incest, adultery, and treason, and if those charges didn't work he was prepared to accuse her of witch-craft – anything to clear the way for his marriage to wife number three, Jane Seymour; Anne was convicted and beheaded in 1536; Henry married Seymour less than two weeks later

unless you really want to . . . Oh, I just sat

In the spring of 1943, during World War II,
British intelligence officers came up with
an unusual scheme to confuse the German
high command: They planted fake top-secret
documents on the corpse of an ordinary soldier
who had recently died of pneumonia, dressed the
body to make it look like a diplomatic courier,
and then dropped it, with a life jacket, off the
coast of Spain in hopes it would be picked up by
the Germans, who would doubtless study (and
hopefully believe) the trumped-up documents it
was carrying. The plan was meant to deceive
German forces into thinking that the Allied
attack on Europe would occur at Sardinia, not
Sicily. To make the corpse as convincing as

possible, it was supplied with identification papers, as well as a photograph of a supposed fiancée, tickets from a recent hit play in London, and a bill of sale from a British jewellery store for a recently purchased engagement ring. The ruse worked. The corpse was picked up by Spanish fishermen, and its papers were carefully pored over by German authorities. Shortly afterward, the German army began sending troops to Sardinia. When Allied forces actually landed at Sicily, they were able to overcome the meagre German defences there. The ingenious plan became the basis of a popular book and movie, *The Man Who Never Was*, in the 1950s.

Beginning in 1949, the CIA gave LSD to dozens of unwitting human subjects as part of illegal experiments to study brainwashing and mind-control techniques. Despite international agreements banning such experimentation (agreements that arose from the horrifying 'medical' experiments conducted by the Nazis in concentration camps), the CIA studies continued, without restriction and without accountability, for more than twenty years. In one instance, a renowned army biochemist, Dr. Frank Olson, was given LSD; he committed suicide by leaping to his death from a tenth-floor window two weeks later. Olson's family was never told the actual circumstances of his death; they didn't learn the truth until 1975 when they happened to read a government report on covert CIA activities. On other occasions, the CIA also studied the effects of LSD and other mind-altering drugs on federal prisoners, hospital nurses, inmates at a psychiatric institution, and ordinary individuals plucked from the street and lured, unaware, into experiments by CIA-paid prostitutes.

'Approximately 80 percent of our air pollution stems from hydrocarbons released by vegetation, so let's not go overboard in setting and enforcing tough emission standards from manmade sources.

– President Ronald Reagan, claiming that trees cause more air pollution than cars, to the delight of his many campaign contributors in the automobile industry, 1981

**'That couldn't take place in
New York City.'**

– Former New York City Mayor Ed Koch, on
a 1988 tour of Europe, expressing disapproval
over the open sale of illegal drugs on the streets
of Amsterdam

'The *Saturday Evening Post* Founded AD 1728 by Benj. Franklin'

– Masthead appearing on the cover of every *Saturday Evening Post*, from 1899 to the present; in actuality, Franklin had nothing to do with the magazine's founding: The first issue appeared thirty years after his death. The misleading masthead was the brainchild of *Post* publisher George Lorimer, who added it to the magazine's cover in 1899 to boost circulation; the magazine's Table of Contents page features a dignified cameo portrait of Franklin as well

'I AM BLIND. PLEASE HELP ME.'

– Sign posted next to 'Blind Charley,' a well-known beggar who stationed himself for years outside Macy's department store in New York City; Charley, who wasn't blind at all, regarded begging as just another job; according to police, he was eventually able to use his street earnings to make various modest real estate investments throughout the city

To the dozens of love-hungry men who called
a Nevada phone sex line in the early 1990s, the
beguiling woman named 'Raven' was a dream
come true. With her velvet voice and sensual
charm, she aroused not just bedroom fantasies
but thoughts of candlelit dinners and romance.
At least one man proposed to her over the
telephone. Others sent love letters. One caller
became so infatuated he called her more than
two dozen times a day. It disappointed all of
them when, only eight months after she'd
started, 'Raven' abruptly quit. The company she
worked for, she complained, was slow to give
out raises and promotions despite her popularity.

It was, she asserted, a simple case of sex discrim-
ination: 'Raven,' unknown to her many phone
fans, was a man, a National Guardsman, married
with four children. His name was Darryl
Malone. 'I had to feed my family,' Malone
explained, when asked why he had taken the
work. His wife – impressed by his gift for female
vocal mimicry – had first suggested the job. 'You
must be wondering,' he later told the press, 'how
an ex-marine could talk sex to men. . . . Who
would be better for the job, since a man knows
what a man wants?'

'We are a fact-gathering organization only. . . . We don't condemn anybody.'

– Former FBI director J. Edgar Hoover; Hoover – who ran the bureau from 1924 to 1972 – was notorious for compiling secret files on the intimate sex lives of prominent U.S. citizens, and then using the information to harass and threaten those individuals – such as Martin Luther King, Jr. – whose politics or lifestyles he personally abhorred

'Pay equalization concept.'

– Term publicly used by the U.S. Senate to refer to a $23,000-per-year pay raise it voted itself in 1991

'I don't know of any authoritative figures that there are hungry children. . . . I think some people are going to soup kitchens voluntarily. I know we've had considerable information that people go to soup kitchens because the food is free and that that's easier than paying for it. . . . I think that they have the money.'

– Reagan White House counsellor Edwin Meese,
dismissing the notion that there is any poverty
or hunger in America, 1983; Meese's remarks
– and his defence one week later of Ebenezer
Scrooge as a fair and equitable employer
('If you really look at the facts, he didn't exploit
Bob Cratchit') – drew the ire of even such
conservative columnists as William Safire

Naturalist and illustrator John James Audubon routinely lied about both the year and the place of his birth. Audubon claimed to have been born in 1780 in New Orleans. In fact, he was born in 1785 in Haiti. The lie was an attempt to obscure the actual circumstances of his birth – he was born out of wedlock, the son of a French naval officer and a Creole servant – and the fact that he was half black. At the time, both issues carried substantial potential for social ostracism.

In 1917, famed newspaper editor and columnist H. L. Mencken – renowned for his acidic sense of humor – wrote a column for the *New York Evening Mail* innocently titled 'A Neglected Anniversary,' in which he purported to describe the history of the bath, from its inception in Cincinnati in 1842 to its indispensability in the early twentieth century. He explained that physicians across the country had originally denounced the bath as a health menace, a contributing factor in the spread of pneumonia, influenza, and other diseases, and that they'd once persuaded cities such as Boston and Philadelphia to outlaw their use. He also casually noted that Millard Fillmore was the first U.S. president to

install a bath in the White House. The article –
a complete and total fabrication from beginning
to end, written (Mencken later insisted) as a
lighthearted joke – was taken seriously by the
public, and Mencken was amazed to see many of
his bath 'facts' eventually reiterated by encyclo-
pedias, history books, members of Congress, and
physicians. Mencken publicly retracted the story
twice, but it did little good. Portions of his bath
'history' continued to appear in various places,
including scholarly journals, for decades. Even
as late as the 1950s, President Harry Truman
was proudly explaining to guests that the very
first bath in the White House had been installed
by Millard Fillmore.

⚕

'THE ALIEN: WORLD'S FIRST AUTHENTIC PHOTOGRAPH'

– September 1996 *Penthouse* magazine cover blurb, hyping what it earnestly described as 'evidence of extraterrestrial visitors to our planet'; despite publisher Bob Guccione's claims that the grainy photos – of an alleged alien humanoid on a hospital gurney – were comparable to 'a photograph of Jesus Christ,' the pictures were later revealed to be of a dummy used as a prop in a 1994 flying saucer movie

'WORLD'S OLDEST NEWSPAPER "GIRL", 101, QUITS BECAUSE SHE'S PREGNANT'

– 1990 headline on a copy of the supermarket tabloid, the *Sun*; the article, a totally spurious story of a 101-year-old woman impregnated by a millionaire on her newspaper route, was accompanied by a photo, which turned out to be of an actual elderly newspaper "girl", ninety-six-year-old Nellie Mitchell, who had been delivering the *Arkansas Gazette* for fifty years; Mitchell, aghast at seeing a photo of herself with the fictitious story, sued the tabloid and was awarded more than $1 million in damages

crying like that . . . Anyone can grow up to be

The 1931 children's film *Skippy* – about two boys and a lovable dog – required its star, child actor Jackie Cooper, to cry profusely in not just one scene but three. The ten-year-old Cooper sometimes found it difficult to oblige, especially toward the end of the shooting schedule, when he was feeling tired and cranky. Director Norman Taurog (Cooper's uncle in real life) eventually reached the end of his patience and warned Cooper that if he didn't start crying for the camera immediately, the film's canine star would be taken outside and shot. Cooper remained obstinate. Finally, Taurog had the dog removed, and a moment later there was the sound of a gun firing. A guilt-stricken Cooper began sobbing uncontrollably – as the cameras rolled and Taurog beamed with satisfaction. Only after Taurog had gotten all the footage he wanted did he reveal he'd been lying: The dog, still alive, was brought back onto the set. Taurog won an Academy Award for Best Director for the film.

'The public safety is menaced and lives and property are in peril . . . Circumstances . . . have created general alarm and terror.'

– Excuse used by the U.S. government to seize control of the Hawaiian Islands in 1893; in actuality, Hawaii's queen, Liliuokalani, was planning reforms that would have substantially diminished encroaching American influence and business interests on the islands; she was quickly deposed by U.S. military forces and, not surprisingly, Sanford Dole – of the Dole pineapple empire – was placed in charge of the islands

'I am not the monster . . .
I am the victim.'

– Former Gestapo officer Adolf Eichmann,
a member of Hitler's power elite, testifying at
his war crimes trial in 1960; Eichmann, who ran
the Nazi bureau for 'Jewish affairs' and who
engineered the slaughter of millions in the
concentration camps, claimed he was little more
than a railway official; he was found guilty of all
the charges against him and was hanged in 1962

'I do not know; am I my brother's keeper?'

– Cain, denying any knowledge of the where-abouts of his brother, Abel, after killing him (Genesis 4:9)

⚸

'Now I didn't come here to talk nonsense about me, Rhett. I came because I was miserable at the thought of you in trouble. . . . In a minute, I *shall* cry.

– Scarlett O'Hara – arrayed in what used to be the green velvet drapes in her parlour – using lies to try to wheedle out of Rhett Butler the money to save Tara from carpetbaggers, in the film *Gone With the Wind* (1939)

'We are sending you out as a matter of precaution. We hope you will be back for breakfast.'

– Lie by which an unknown officer on the
Titanic tried to ease the anxiety of fifty-year-old
passenger Elizabeth Lines and her sixteen-year-
old daughter, Mary, while persuading them to
get into one of the lifeboats; both women were
among the rescued

In the early morning hours of December 3, 1984, a giant white cloud of methyl isocyanate, a deadly pesticide gas, wafted without warning through the city of Bhopal, India, instantly incapacitating hundreds of thousands of residents and eventually killing nearly 17,000 of them. The cloud – which had escaped from a nearby Union Carbide chemical processing plant – was so lethal that hundreds of people were dead even before an alarm could be sounded; the cloud travelled for miles, leaving in its wake a landscape of screaming or unconscious humans and animals. Reacting to angry criticism that such a hazardous plant should never have been built in the middle of a heavily populated area, a spokesman for Union Carbide claimed that the region had originally been sparsely populated, but that it later became congested as a result of the plant's presence. 'There is a tendency in India,' he insisted, 'for people to gravitate toward commercial activity, even a chemical plant.' Detractors of the explanation noted that Bhopal had been a major population center since the eighteenth century and that, at the time of the plant's construction, the population of the area was almost five million.

'WITCH FINDER GENERAL'

– Self-anointed title of seventeenth-century European con man Matthew Hopkins, who toured the English countryside and charged exorbitant sums to rid villages of alleged witches and wizards; Hopkins's methods – which virtually always guaranteed that anyone he suspected of witchcraft would be found guilty (he was, after all, paid on a 'per witch' basis) – led to the torture and execution of more than 230 innocent women and men; in 1647, he was finally exposed as a murderous charlatan and was lynched

'School? Well, I – uh, I was going to school till I met somebody. Yeah! Uh – two big monsters. And – and they tied me in a big sack!'

– Pinocchio, lying for the very first time, and discovering that his nose grows very, very long

⚶

'I do not know the man.'

– Peter, denying his association with Jesus, not once but three times, after Jesus' arrest in the Garden of Gethsemane (Matthew 26:72)

———◆———

If you would like more information on the full list of humour titles published by Michael O'Mara Books Limited please contact our UK sales department on:

fax: 0171 622 6956
email: *jokes@michaelomarabooks.com*

Titles include:
- The Complete History of Farting
- The World's Greatest Lies
- On Second Thoughts
- Bitch!
- The Stupidest Things Ever Said
- The Stupidest Things Ever Done
- Stupid Sex
- The Nastiest Things Ever Said